D0547458

The Hard Problem

Tom Stoppard's work includes *Rosencrantz and Guildenstern Are Dead*, *The Real Inspector Hound*, *Jumpers*, *Travesties*, *Night and Day*, *Every Good Boy Deserves Favour*, *After Magritte*, *Dirty Linen*, *The Real Thing*, *Hapgood*, *Arcadia*, *Indian Ink*, *The Invention of Love*, the trilogy *The Coast of Utopia* and *Rock 'n' Roll*. His radio plays include *If You're Glad I'll Be Frank*, *Albert's Bridge*, *Where Are They Now?*, *Artist Descending a Staircase*, *The Dog It Was That Died*, *In the Native State* and *Darkside* (incorporating Pink Floyd's *Dark Side of the Moon*). Television work includes *Professional Foul*, *Squaring the Circle* and *Parade's End*. His film credits include *Empire of the Sun*, *Rosencrantz and Guildenstern Are Dead*, which he also directed, *Shakespeare in Love*, *Enigma* and *Anna Karenina*.

also by Tom Stoppard

TOM STOPPARD

The Hard Problem

ff

FABER & FABER

First published in 2015
by Faber and Faber Limited
74–77 Great Russell Street, London WC1B 3DA

Typeset by Country Setting, Kingsdown, Kent CT14 8ES

A CIP record for this book is available from the British Library

ISBN
978–0–571–32292–3 (hbk)
978–0–571–32293–0 (pbk)
978–0–571–32295–4 (limited edn)

FSC
www.fsc.org
MIX
Paper from
responsible sources
FSC® C101712

2 4 6 8 10 9 7 5 3 1

For Sabrina

Author's Note

I am grateful for help from the British Association for Adoption and Fostering, in the person of Dr John Simmonds. It is my responsibility that the circumstances in the play have more regard for dramatic purpose than for contemporary regulations.

As for the science in *The Hard Problem*, I am in debt to more books than I can mention, and I have also enjoyed the privilege of exchanges with John Coates (whose recent work on hormone-related performance in the financial world the plot anticipates), Richard Dawkins, Robert May, Thomas Nagel, John Searle, Elliott Sober, George Sugihara and David Sloan Wilson. I owe particular thanks to Armand Marie Leroi who was a patient guide through the writing and saved me from numerous errors.

The Hard Problem was first produced on the Dorfman stage of the National Theatre, London, on 21 January 2015. The cast in order of speaking was as follows:

Spike Damien Molony
Hilary Olivia Vinall
Amal Parth Thakerar
Leo Jonathan Coy
Julia Rosie Hilal
Ursula Lucy Robinson
Jerry Anthony Calf
Cathy Hayley Canham / Daisy Jacob / Eloise Webb
Bo Vera Chok

Director Nicholas Hytner
Designer Bob Crowley
Lighting Designer Mark Henderson
Sound Designer Paul Arditti
Company Voice Work Jeannette Nelson
Staff Director Zachary James

Characters

Spike

Hilary

Amal

Leo

Julia

Ursula

Jerry

Cathy

Bo

THE HARD PROBLEM

SCENE ONE

Hilary's bedsit. Evening.
   Hilary, twenty-two, and Spike, about thirty, with mugs of coffee.

Spike You're looking at two years. The jewellery was under the floorboards. The police have nothing to connect you to the scene of the robbery.

Hilary I'm going to vomit.

Spike If you stick to the story, they can only charge you with receiving. With good behaviour, you'll be out in a year. On the other hand –

   Hilary performs exaggerated boredom, a collapse of unloosened joints.

Hilary I'm warning you, Spike. Projectile vomiting. If I hear the words 'prisoner's dilemma', I'm not going to make it to the toilet.

Spike You're being childish. The Krohl is a plum ticket and the psychology department has published a dozen papers on the Dilemma, so hang in. The question is, can you trust Bob?

Hilary Who's Bob?

Spike *Bob* is who smashed the jeweller's window while you grabbed the rings and watches.

Hilary Oh, *Bob*.

Spike *Bob* is who's sticking to the story, you hope. *Bob* is who's asking himself, can I trust Luanne to stick to the story?

3

Hilary *Luanne?*

Spike There's never been a smash-and-grab jewel raider called Hilary. If Bob turns state's evidence he'll get off and you'll get seven years because you stuck to the story, you muggins.

Hilary Why would Bob do that except in the Ladybird Book of Game Theory?

Spike In case you do it to him. That's what this is about. That's why the game is called the prisoner's dilemma. Two rational prisoners will betray each other even though they know they would have done better to trust each other.

Hilary Rational? You have to be a *person* to be rational. You've left out everything about Bob and me except we're each out for ourselves and we've got two buttons to push. Actually, Bob loves me.

Spike Hold on.

Hilary I did it. Bob had nothing to do with it, he wasn't even there.

Spike That's not one of the options.

Hilary I smashed the window, grabbed the jewellery and hid it under the floorboards.

Spike It's not an option in the game.

Hilary I'm confessing anyway. I'm going to give Bob a chance to go straight.

Spike (*beat*) Why?

Hilary Because I'm good.

Spike Right. Promise me one thing. Don't pull this one if it comes up in your interview. The game is not about you and Bob, it's about a statistical tendency. It's about survival strategies hard-wired into our brains millions of years ago. Who eats, who gets eaten, who gets to advance their genes into the next generation. Competition is the natural order. Self-interest is bedrock. Co-operation is a strategy. Altruism is an outlier unless you're an ant or a bee. You're not an ant or a bee, you're competing to do a doctorate at the Krohl Institute where they're basically seeing first-class honours degrees and you're in line for a two-one, so don't be a smart arse, and above all don't use the word good as though it meant something in evolutionary science.

Spike tastes his coffee.

Horrible. Haven't you even got sweetener?

Hilary Don't you believe in good, Spike?

Spike I believe in it, it's just not what you think it is.

Hilary What do you think it is?

Spike Behaviour. It takes millions of years to evolve, but it's evolved behaviour, whether you're a person or a vampire bat. Every night, vampire bats leave the cave in search of warm blood. When they get back to the cave, the ones who were lucky cough up for the ones who weren't. Literally. They regurgitate some of the blood to feed the bats who came home hungry. Do you think these are *good* vampire bats?

Hilary No. I don't. But I don't think they're little people with wings and sonar, either.

Spike I didn't want to be the one to break it to you. How many times do you think a bat will refuse to share its dinner before it finds out next time it comes home hungry the other bats won't cough up?

Hilary I don't know.

5

Spike I don't know either, but off the top of my head . . . four. Four times, say. That'll teach the selfish little bastard how to behave. I don't see that we have much to feel superior about, as a species. Altruism is always self-interest, it just needs a little working out.

Hilary Like you going miles out of your way to give me a lift home?

Spike Exactly. It's a cost-benefit thing. I go miles out of my way because you might invite me in for coffee, and I throw in a tutorial to get into your –

Hilary Pants.

Spike – good graces, I was going to say. But you're basically right on the biology.

Hilary I'd rather not complicate . . .

Spike Hey, I'm your tutor, it would be an abuse of trust without precedent in higher education.

Hilary It's a cost-benefit thing. I'm sorry about the coffee, too. But giving something to get something isn't altruism, anyway.

Spike That's what I'm saying.

Hilary No, you're not, you're saying there's no such thing, and I'm saying there is. I'm saying Rose of Sharon giving her milk to a starving man is different from bats.

Spike Rose of Sharon. Is she in the Bible?

Hilary No, she's in *The Grapes of Wrath*, you pillock.

Spike Oh, fiction. If you want a tip, don't cite works of fiction.

Hilary Rose of Sharon's baby is born dead, so she gives her breast to an old man dying of hunger, a stranger, just some old man they find lying in a barn where the family are sheltering from the rainstorm. That's how the story ends, with Rosasharn holding a starving man to her breast. Altruism means being good for its own sake.

Spike Didn't it make her feel better, though, about her life, her baby, didn't it give her the courage to go on, and have more babies?

Hilary (*beat*) Fuck you, Spike.

Spike (*laughs*) Darwin doesn't do sentimental. If you want something cuddly, try business studies. Here, there's nothing but evolutionary biology. Breastfeeding a starving man? Evo-bio. The Good Samaritan? Evo-bio. Culture, empathy, faith, hope and charity, all the flip-sides of egoism, come back to biology, because there just ain't anywhere else to come from except three pounds of grey matter wired up in your head like a map of the London Underground with eighty six billion stations connected thirty trillion ways, hard-wired for me first. How many times do you think I'd drive you home for a mug of what isn't even proper coffee before I give up on the sweetener and let you go home on the bus?

Hilary Four?

Spike Yeah. At least.

Hilary At *least*?

Spike Yes. At least four.

He tries another mouthful of coffee, grimaces, and picks up his outdoor coat.

Hilary Oh.

She considers him. He offers a handshake and leaves. She starts getting undressed.

SCENE TWO

Night. The only light is from a 'scented'-type candle by the bed.

Hilary is kneeling silently at the side of her bed, saying her prayers. She is wearing only a T-shirt, which is long enough for modesty.

Spike pushes open the door, letting in more light. He enters with a mug in each hand. He is barefoot, wearing a girly wrap-over negligee too small for him, showing bare calves. Seeing Hilary at her prayers, he is dumbfounded. He hesitates, not sure what to do. He decides to leave and make a later entrance, but Hilary suddenly relaxes, stands up and gets into the crumpled bed, unbothered by seeing Spike.

The clothes they have taken off are untidily 'anywhere'.

Spike Sorry.

Hilary What (*about*)?

Spike Were you *praying*?

Hilary Yes.

Spike Sorry if I came in at the wrong moment.

Hilary I was saying my prayers, I wasn't putting in my dentures. (*Accepting the mug.*) Thanks.

Spike I'm glad you did that after, not before.

Hilary I feel the same way about what you're wearing.

They each take a sip and wordlessly exchange mugs. Spike gets into bed beside her.

Spike You're lovely. It was lovely. Afterwards, you said – muttered really, did you know? – you said, 'Thank you.' 'Thank you'. I thought that was so . . . You don't have to say thank you.

Hilary Actually, I wasn't talking to you.

Spike Oh. Sorry.
So . . . so you, as it were, pray to God, then?

Hilary Yes.

Spike Do you pray every night?

Hilary Yes. Usually before I get into bed.

Spike Oh.
Does it work?

Hilary Yes.

Spike (*interested*) You find prayer works?

Hilary Yes.

Spike What, every time?

Hilary Yes. Every time I say my prayers I feel better.

Spike Oh, *works*, right. Psychological.

Hilary Wow, Spike, I never thought of that, missed it completely, shit, that explains it. (*Wagging her hand in front of his face.*) Hello, hello. When I clap my hands you will wake up and find you're in bed with a student, wearing a negligee.

Spike Lucky me. Better than when? What do you pray for?

Hilary Forgiveness.

Spike Forgiveness? I thought it was me who should be doing that. What you need to pray for is getting into the Krohl Institute. How does God feel about your model of Nature–Nurture Convergence in Egoistic and Altruistic Parent–Offspring Behaviour? Does he think you're on the right lines?

Hilary I tell you what, Spike, if I were up for a back-and-forth about God, I'd rather not have it with an arsehole. Where we were –

She turns on her bedside light.

– was, you were supposed to be checking the maths for me.

Spike To tell you the truth, I feel a bit thrown now. I wasn't expecting to deal with a rival hypothesis.

Hilary That's not what I said. *I'm* not thrown by sharing an ancestor with a grunting chimpanzee – evolution by natural selection, bring it on – it's only that millions of years later the chimp is still grunting and you're using words like hypothesis, so I'm wondering if there's something they left out. It's nothing for you to be bothered by.

Spike (*roused*) If not me, who? I'm Darwin. I'm Mendel. I'm Crick and Watson. I stand for all the science that's taught. We've scraped you clean of gibberish, we've taken you to bits and put you back together from the atoms upwards so you understand how you work and how everything around you works. We've accounted for every particle in the universe except for dark matter, and we're working on that. And here you are on your knees to what? To who? You might as well pray to Peter Rabbit.

Hilary Explain consciousness.

Spike Apart from consciousness. (*Silly voice.*) 'Explain consciousness.' There's no baby, there's only bathwater. (*Getting angrier.*) I've got nothing personal against God, except the usual, but I expected better from you. When did your mind turn into a party balloon? You made it nearly to the end of the journey, give it a few more years and we'll have gravity wrapped in with the other forces, and there'll be nothing for science to do except collect new beetles – well, I don't believe that entirely, in fact I'm so disgusted I've started talking bollocks.

Hilary Explain consciousness.

Impatiently, Spike takes her finger and holds it to the flame of the candle for a moment before she snatches it away with a little gasp.

Spike Flame – finger – brain; brain – finger – ouch. Consciousness.

Hilary Brilliant. Now do sorrow.

Spike groans.

You think you've done pain. If you wired me up you could track the signal, zip-zip. If you put my brain in a scanner you could locate the activity. *Ping!* Pain! Now do sorrow. How do I feel sorrow?

Spike Do you feel sorrow?

Hilary Yes.

Spike I'm making you sad?

Hilary Not everything is about you, Spike.

Spike Right.

He gets out of bed and goes to sit at the table, where there is a laptop. He opens the laptop and taps keys.

Hilary Scaredy-cat! You can explain the *mechanics*. You should work in a garage. (*Garage voice.*) 'It's yer big end's gone, mate. Does it hurt when I do this?', and answer came there none, because it's a bloody *car*!

Spike ignores her, studies the computer screen thoughtfully, scrolling.

I don't go looking for an argument with science. Tell me my DNA is seventy per cent banana, and I think, well, fine, there are more things in heaven and earth than are dreamt of in your philosophy, Hilary. But with *consciousness* – with the mind–body problem – the God idea shoves itself to the front like a doctor at the scene of an accident, because when you come right down to it, the body is made of *things*, and things don't have thoughts. Bananas aren't thinking, 'Hey, seven eights is fifty-six', or 'I'm not the king of Spain', and when you take a banana to bits you can see why.

Spike Don't publish till you hear back from the Krohl.

Hilary (*persisting*) Same with brains. The mind is extra.

Spike The human brain, for its size, is the most complex –

Hilary does her boredom collapse.

Hilary – object on the planet, in the galaxy, the universe – forget it, Spike, I've got the T-shirt. If organising enough components the right way is all it takes, maybe a thermostat is a kiddie-step towards being conscious –

Spike (Maybe.)

Hilary – which is what I'm reading. Did you say maybe?

Spike I don't see anything obviously wrong with that.

Hilary You believe a thermostat has consciousness potential, but you find God a bit of a stretch?

Spike (*tapping*) Uh-huh, but you should stick with God – your way with an equation would need his collaboration.

Hilary laughs, giving up.

Hilary That's what you're here for. God can only do so much. I put in for six research slots in industry, plus Imperial for the hell of it and the Krohl for sheer cheek, and only the Krohl has offered me an interview.

Spike The Krohl didn't know about your maths.

Hilary I'm not even doing what I'd call brain science.

Spike You must be. Seeing as it's the Krohl Institute for Brain Science. Which means neurobio, neuropsycho, neuro-everything, plus its own gym, organic vegetables and free pilates, I'm told, all paid for by a squillionaire with a Master's in biophysics who decided to try hedge-funding . . . which raises the interesting question: is Krohl an altruist or an egoist? (*Garage voice.*) 'What you've got here is a wonky co-variance, miss.'

Hilary hurriedly gets out of bed and goes to look over his shoulder.

Hilary (*worried*) What's wrong with it?

Spike The model works okay for behaviour one on one in an idealised sort of way, think Raphael's *Madonna and Child*, which I personally call 'Woman Maximising Gene Survival', but it won't generalise, because you haven't allowed for future offspring, and if they have different fathers, you'll need to differentiate –

Hilary Can you fix it by Wednesday?

Spike (*garage voice*) 'Do my best, miss, but I'll have to strip her right down to get at it.' (*Normal voice.*) And that's just the customer.

He reaches behind him. She swipes his hand away.

Hilary Can you?

Spike Also, it's not good science to call mother love a virtue, or even mother love.

Hilary You don't think mother love is a virtue?

Spike You don't *call* it a virtue, because at root its virtue consists in its utility.

Hilary Utility. *Mother love?*

Spike Genetically selected behaviour to maximise –

Hilary Spike, do you know anyone who believes that, really and truly?

Spike I don't know anyone who *doesn't* believe it. Parental behaviour. Hard-wired when we were roaming the savannah in small groups of hunter-gatherers. Mother and baby are in a cost-benefit competition. Have you ever seen a newborn infant screaming to be fed? – the *anger* – the *noise* – the *face* . . .! The kid is laying it on, and it probably started in the womb.

Hilary (*flaring up*) Oh, probably! The kid doesn't know up from down but it knows to maximise the survival of its genes! And Mummy's genes are working out the odds of their survival in the baby, against her chances of having more kids. It's a cost-benefit competition, and the genes, unlike some of us, can do the maths, is that right?

Spike Well –

Hilary Just shut up!

Pause.

Spike It's not personal.

Pause.

Obviously, genes have no *intentions*, it's *as if*; it's a metaphor.

Hilary A metaphor for what?

Spike A reflex. A survival reflex.

Hilary Genes don't have a survival *problem*, Spike, they're *genes*. They're little tiny *things*, like, I don't know, molecules! *Metaphorically*, genes want to hop the next train before the train they're on conks out, *'as if'* they know life has a value which extinction doesn't have, but the science has no underneath, it's tortoises all the way down. I agree with you, Spike. Virtue is not science. You can't get an *ought* out of an *is*. Morality is not science. So there must be something else, which isn't science. Which science isn't. What is it?

Spike Wait.

He brings a bucket-sized bin from under the table and places it on the table in front of her, and stands back.

Moral rules are the stable strategy evolved by millions of years of jockeying between humans in real-life situations like the game of prisoner's dilemma.

The bin is Spike's 'joke'. Hilary humours him. She pretends to retch into the bin.

(*Solicitously.*) That's right. Better out than in.

Hilary straightens up with the bin over her head. She stands there like that.

You don't like the idea that you're nothing else but an animal. It's conceit. You're an animal. Get over it.

She doesn't answer. Spike watches her. She doesn't do anything. After a while he realises she is crying inside the bin.

Hilly . . .

She starts to bawl inside the bin. Concerned, he goes round the table to her.

What?!

Aware that he is close, she moves away from him a little, sobbing loudly. Spike waits for her to subside. Finally, she takes the bin off her head and puts it under the table.

What happened?

Hilary Nothing happened. I'm okay, Spike.

Spike Of course you are. It'll be fine.

Hilary Oh, that. Forget that.

She closes the laptop.

(*Laughs.*) I need a miracle.

SCENE THREE

The Krohl Institute for Brain Science is a purpose-built complex of labs and offices on which no expense has been spared, set in its own grounds. It employs perhaps 150 people. Something of the expense and scale is suggested by what we see, which is a mere fragment of the whole, a walk-through/waiting area. Everyone we get to see has a security pass (with photo) worn around the neck, specific to the bearer. This is true of all scenes set in the Institute.

Hilary, dressed for the interview, with a laptop bag and an old satchel, sits waiting in a designer chair. Specialist periodicals and print-outs encased in Krohl-branded file-holders are available, and perhaps a wall-mounted computer screen silently offers more material. Hilary turns over pages, looking up briefly when a woman, of Hilary's age, crosses the space. The woman (Julia) hesitates slightly as she takes a second look at Hilary, and continues on her way, and is followed in, more tentatively, by a young man, Amal, wearing a cheap suit and carrying a haversack. He is Indian. He sits down near Hilary.

Amal Hi.

Hilary Hi.

Amal chooses a print-out to look at. Hilary sizes him up. He catches her eye.

Amal Are you here for an interview?

Hilary (*nods*) Dr Reinhart

Amal Same here. What time . . .?

Hilary Eleven-fifteen.

Amal It's nearly twelve.

Hilary I know.

Amal Maybe he forgot about you.

Hilary Is your doctorate in psychology?

Amal If necessary. My degree is in maths, and I'm doing
a Master's in biophysics, which is actually a neurobiology
research project I managed to latch on to, to make myself
beautiful for the Krohl! We already published a paper
which I've got my name on. I'm Amal, by the way.

Hilary Hilary. Wow.

Amal How about you?

Hilary Yes. Psychology. I haven't graduated yet. So you
liked the Krohl Institute?

Amal What's not? It's small, it's not industry, it's not
academia, it's state of the art for imaging and all the toys,
it's elitist but in a good way, it's got a gym, and after five
years of Cambridge it's not in Cambridge.

Hilary Oh.

Amal Where are you?

Hilary Loughborough.

Amal Where's that?

Hilary Loughborough.
We must be up for the same job.

Amal Well, good luck.

Hilary I'll say.

Amal (?)

Hilary Thank you. Good luck to you, too.

Amal Thanks. Psychology is a sideshow at the Krohl. You need a hard-science crossover to improve your chances – a lot of what they publish is on mice and macaques.

Hilary (*surprised*) Parrots?

Amal Monkeys.

Hilary Oh, right.

Amal Monkeys are great. Scan the hell out of them, open up their little heads, try this, try that, see what happens, and they don't sue.

Hilary Yeah, that wouldn't work with behavioural psychology.

Amal I've submitted to do an experiment tracking unconscious readiness potential move by move in two subjects playing a repeated prisoner's dilemma.

Hilary They're going to love you.

Amal It's just to get me through the door. The Dilemma is cleaned out, it was oversold in the first place with the one-shot game –

Hilary (*pleased*) That's just what I . . .

Amal I wonder what's happened to our . . .?

Hilary Perhaps this is it. *Candid Camera.*

Amal Do you think so?

Made uneasy, he corrects his sprawl. They fall silent. Leo enters. He's running late but unfussed.

Leo Apologies. I'm Leo Reinhart.

Hilary and Amal stand up.

Which of you is my eleven-fifteen?

Hilary I am, sir. Hilary Matthews.

Leo Then you must be my twelve o'clock.

Amal Amal Admati.

Leo I have to ask you a favour, Hilary. I can save a few minutes if I take Amal first.

Hilary (Of course.)

Leo So, Amal, come with me and tell me why you believe a machine can think, or why you believe it can't, whichever you prefer.

Amal grabs his haversack and follows Leo out.

Amal (*leaving*) Can a machine think . . . ?

Hilary takes out her laptop, opens it, gets something up, looks at it, despairs of it, closes the laptop.
Julia enters and goes straight to Hilary.

Julia Hilary . . . I knew it was you. Do you remember me? It's Julia. Redcliffs High. The Purple Gang!

Hilary Julia . . . Julia Chamberlain. Gosh. Hello! Do you work here?

Julia Yes, nothing brainy, surprise, surprise! I do a pilates class for who wants it. My partner works here, she's the brainy one. You'll meet her in a minute. How are things with you, Hilary?

Hilary Fine. Thanks. The Purple Gang! Do you hear from anyone?

Julia Christmas cards. Not really. What did you do after Redcliffs?

Hilary I had the baby.

Julia Oh, I wasn't asking . . .!

Hilary It's all right.

Julia The Head told us, just the seniors.

Hilary Awful warning, was I?

Julia No, honestly, she was really sympathetic. She said you might come back to do your GCSEs.

Hilary I suppose that's what girls do now, with a bucket under the desk.

Julia Mm, not at Redcliffs. What was your baby?

Hilary A girl. Catherine. I don't know if she's still Catherine. You don't get to know. Anything. She was six in November. Guy Fawkes night! The sky was exploding.

Julia Oh, Hilly.

Hilary Yes. Well. You know. The adoption was all arranged beforehand. No granny, and my poor dad wasn't about to take it in his stride. I was quite relieved, actually. I wasn't into babies. It was different when it came to it. But, I don't know, everything just went ahead, it seemed like the best thing.

Julia What about the, your, well, boyfriend, was he?

Hilary I didn't have a boyfriend. It was stupider than that. I never saw him again, and didn't much want to. Really stupid.

Julia But here you are.

Hilary (*nods*) Reading psychology at Loughborough.

Julia So everything turned out all right.
I'm sorry. I'm an idiot. Here's Ursula coming. Listen, good luck.

Ursula approaches.

Ursula, look! – Hilary Matthews.

Ursula Hello. Ursula Tarrant.

Julia Hilary's here for her interview.

Hilary I was amazed. I think it must be a mistake.

Ursula Usually is, but picking a winner from the slush pile is Leo's little vanity. Sorry, that sounds rude. I bet your application was brilliant. How did you get on?

Hilary I haven't had it yet . . . Dr Reinhart is in there with the other candidate.

Ursula The men's room? That could be good. It could be bad. Hard to tell. What's the competition?

Hilary Mathematician. He's Indian.

Ursula Ooh, that's bad.

Hilary I know.

Ursula Where's your degree?

Hilary Loughborough.

Ursula That's definitely good. That's inclusive, Loughborough. The intake here is way too up itself.

Julia Don't mind Ursula.

Hilary Oh, I don't! God, I wish I had an earthly now! I wish my model had a neurobiology crossover –

Ursula Forget your model, he just wants to hear what you're thinking. Good luck.

Julia Come to the gym after if you can.

Hilary nods.

Ursula makes to leave with Julia but changes her mind and comes back, close to Hilary, more intimately. Julia pauses to watch.

Ursula He doesn't like neurobiology. Obviously he likes it, but it's not what he *likes*, do you see?

Hilary No.

Ursula The Krohl mostly does brains. Matter. But Leo likes minds as the way to go. What he *likes*, what he really, really likes, is the Hard Problem.

Hilary Which hard problem?

Ursula We do brain science. There is only one Hard Problem.

Leo and Amal are returning, already audible.

Hilary (*beat*) Okay.

Ursula goes back to Julia and they leave.
When Leo reappears with Amal he has changed into a tracksuit and tennis shoes. He carries a tennis racket.

Amal . . . Sure, but the brain *is* a machine, a biological machine, and it thinks. It happens to be made of living cells but it would make no difference if the machine was made of electronic gates and circuits, or paperclips and rubber bands for that matter. It just has to be able to compute.

Leo Computers compute. Brains think. Is the machine thinking?

Amal If it's playing chess and you can't tell from the moves if the computer is playing white or black, it's thinking.

Leo What it's doing is a lot of binary operations following the rules of its programming.

Amal So is a brain.

Leo But can a computer do what a brain can do?

Amal Are you kidding? – A brain doesn't come close!

Leo (*to Hilary*) Do you want to jump in?

Hilary Not much.

Leo Really? Why?

Hilary It's not deep. If that's thinking. An adding machine on speed. A two-way switch with a memory. Why *wouldn't* it play chess? But when it's me to move, is the computer *thoughtful* or is it sitting there like a toaster? It's sitting there like a toaster.

Leo So, what would be your idea of deep?

Hilary A computer that minds losing.

Leo takes a moment to reconsider her.

Amal If I made a computer simulating a human brain neuron by neuron, it would mind losing.

Leo (*to Hilary*) Do you agree?

Hilary No.

Leo Amal's machine wouldn't be conscious?

Hilary No, but how would you tell? You can't tell by watching the wheels go round. Just like with a brain. I couldn't tell what you're thinking by watching what your brain is doing, or even that you're thinking.

Amal I'll tell you what I'm thinking. There is overwhelming evidence that the brain causes consciousness.

Hilary There's overwhelming evidence that brain activity correlates with consciousness. Registers consciousness. Nobody's got anywhere trying to show how the brain is conscious.

Amal This is mysticism!

Leo (*to Hilary*) So, how would consciousness come about?

Hilary I have no idea, and nor does anyone else. I thought that's why we're here. To crack the Hard Problem.

Leo (*beat*) It is. It is why we're here. (*Checking his watch, to Amal.*) Thank you. Apologies again.

Jerry, wearing a tracksuit and carrying his racket, enters.

Jerry!
(*To Hilary.*) As you see, I have a pressing engagement. There is an excellent eatery, lavishly subsidised. After lunch, you can hang around in the department and see what's going on.

Leo and Jerry shake hands.

Amal Excuse me!

They stop for him.

Was that my interview? In the toilet?

Leo Yes. Good luck with your career.

They are leaving again.

Amal Good luck with yours!

That stops them again.

I'm sorry, but if you separate what you can't understand from anatomy, you're going backwards to Plato. The brain is physical, and there's no other kind of stuff out there, there's no beans that haven't been counted. The maths to explain what's going on in the brain is like trying to write the equations for a waterfall as big as – I have no idea how big, as big as a million Niagaras maybe – and so far we can write a short-term prediction for two variables in a mixer tap; probably – but the only way to go is to map brain activity in greater and greater detail against conscious experience. There's no hard science in a psychology test if it's not plugged into a brain scan. Neurobiology.

Leo (*pause*) Amal, you're bright, you're going to do fine.

He goes to leave.

Jerry Go ahead, Leo, I'll be right there.

Leo leaves.

(*To Amal.*) I don't think you can write a prediction for a non-linear complex system, even for a mixer tap.

Amal Short term you can, if you have some earlier values for the variables. That gives you a history of the system's behaviour, like a library of the patterns it made, because there *is* a pattern, a chaotic system isn't *really* random, it just *looks* random. So you look in the library for previous states of the system, and where you find some similarity to what you're looking at now, you can expect to see similar behaviour in the short-term future.

Jerry considers this for a couple of beats; accepts it.

Jerry Uh-huh.

Amal You're not the tennis coach, then. Do you work here?

Jerry Not really. I visit. My office is in town. Come and see us.

Amal Oh. Okay.

Jerry What's your name?

Amal Admati, Amal Admati. What's yours?

Jerry It's on the building. But people call me Jerry.

He goes.
    Amal and Hilary stare at each other.

SCENE FOUR

An eleven-year-old girl, Cathy, is having breakfast at one end of a long table which cost, say, £100,000, in an apartment which cost, say, £30 million. A second place is laid by her. Her cereal box is anomalous amid the silver and crystal containing coffee, milk, juice. There are expensive flowers on the table and also a fresh-folded Financial Times.

Jerry enters, laughing into his cell phone. He is five years older. He's wearing chinos and a polo shirt.

Jerry Hey, what a coincidence . . .! Enjoy your dinner, my friend.

He ends the call and, kissing Cathy, sits down.

Morning, Lollipop. How was the birthday party?

He has two phones, one personal, one business. He unfolds the Financial Times, *glancing at a story below the fold.*

Cathy We went on the London Eye, and had pizza and afterwards *The Lion King*.

Jerry (*impressed*) (!)

Cathy Dad, what's coincidence?

Jerry A coincidence? You know what a coincidence is, it's like a long shot . . .

Cathy A long – ?

Jerry . . . No, wait, a coincidence is two things happening at the same time.

Cathy There's lots of things happening at the same time *all* the time.

Jerry That's true. So normally you don't bother to call that a coincidence, but if two things which you don't normally *expect* to happen at the same time, happen at the same time . . .

Cathy Like your friend having dinner when you're having breakfast? You don't expect that.

Jerry You do if he's in Japan, where it's dinnertime. But say you're walking down the street and you bump into your school friend, you'd call that a coincidence, you'd say, 'Fancy seeing you here! What a coincidence!'

Cathy Specially if I was walking down the street in Japan.

Jerry Especially then. You'd say, 'Wow, that's a one-chance-in-a-million coincidence!' But there's reasons why you were both in the same place at the same time, so in another way the million-to-one coincidence had to happen. You just didn't have the information.

Cathy Like what?

Jerry Suppose your school friend was Japanese, and suppose you were both crazy about . . . dinosaurs. Then, maybe, instead of a million times, you'd only have to go to Japan a hundred times before you bumped into her at the dinosaur park in Tokyo. Though I wouldn't bet on it personally.

Cathy I would. I could win a hundred pounds.

Jerry Or lose your pound.

Cathy Hm. Yes.

Jerry You need more information. Everything that makes the coincidence smaller and smaller till you decide it's worth betting your pound, is information.

Cathy Did you have more information?

Jerry Oh, yes.

Cathy Did you bet on your coincidence?

Jerry Oh, yes. In fact, it wasn't really a coincidence any more, and I didn't need to go to Japan.

Cathy Hm. Will you show me how?

Jerry I will.

His phone burps. He glances, cancels it.

Eat up. The car's downstairs and Marie-Cecile has got your bag.

Cathy Can I sit in front with Arthur?

Jerry No, Sam has to sit in front.

Cathy Why?

Jerry Because Sam is in charge, and he wants you in the back with Marie-Cecile.

Cathy Boo. If Mummy says I can, does it mean I can?

Jerry Definitely.

He glances again at the paper. Cathy produces a girly mobile phone, prods at the keys. Jerry accepts a call on his phone. Their voices more or less dovetail.

Hannah, good morning, but that's it, goodbye.

He adds a laugh, then interrupts.

Because I'm not talking to you. You wrote yourself into Siberia.

Cathy (*without preamble*) Can I sit in front with Arthur?

Mummy gives her a blast down the phone. Cathy slumps under the cares of the world, like Hilary doing boredom.

Jerry It was inaccurate online, and you're not looking pretty-in-pink, either.

He tosses aside the Financial Times.

Cathy All right! I was only asking!

Jerry When Krohl Capital calls the top of the market, we won't be calling it in Soho House, you bottom-feeder.

Cathy We went on the London Eye.

Jerry You should have listened to me.

Cathy He's on the phone.

Jerry Have a nice winter.

Cathy Mum . . .

Jerry ends the call, and takes Cathy's phone to talk into.

Rude!

Jerry Hi, sweetheart, don't wait dinner, in fact don't wait up.
Hold on.

(*To Cathy.*) Did you give Sally her present?

Cathy nods.

Yes.
No, I'd rather wake up in the country.

He checks his phone.

Here she is. Big kiss.

Jerry returns Cathy's phone to her, and answers his own.

Cathy Mummy . . .

Jerry Simon.

Cathy Am I an orphan?

Jerry, listening to Simon, reacts to Cathy.

Jerry What?

Cathy (*to phone*) An orphan. Sally said if you're adopted it means you're an orphan.

Jerry Does this look like an orphanage?

His attention returns to his phone. Jerry is not thrown by the interruption, which in no way introduces an emotional note. Cathy's responses are matter-of-fact, casual.

Cathy Uh-huh . . . uh-huh . . .

Jerry So here's what, Simon.

Cathy Uh-huh.

Jerry I'll write you a cheque for a hundred and ten million. Then you can stop worrying about me, and I can stop worrying about you.

Cathy Okay.

Jerry Only, don't ask to come back in.

Cathy (*losing interest*) *Okay.*

Jerry Well, it's your call.

Cathy Uh, pizza. And we went to *The Lion King* . . . (Yes, excellent.) . . .

Jerry Because she's a *journalist*.

Cathy All right, I'll ask him. 'Bye, Mummy.

Jerry I'm gone.

They both end their calls.

(*Mutters.*) Wanker.
  Ask me.

Cathy What?

Jerry Do you want to ask me something?

Cathy Why?

Jerry You said –

Cathy Oh. I have to ask Sam to stop in the village for dog biscuits.

    Beat.

Jerry Dog biscuits. Right.

    He picks up speed.

I've got a meeting with some people coming. Give me a kiss and get going.

Cathy What kind of people?

Jerry People kind. Don't I get a kiss?

    Cathy gives him a kiss.

Cathy Will you show me where you work?

Jerry I will.

Cathy Soon?

Jerry Soon, Cathy. When you find it interesting. But I'll take you to a place I know where there's lots of interesting things, machines, monkeys . . .

Cathy When?

Jerry Next time.

Cathy Okay. 'Bye, Daddy.

Jerry Sayonara.

    Cathy goes. Jerry's phone burps. He looks and listens.

Yeah. No, the dining room. And let me know when my visitors are in the lift.

He closes the call. He empties his cup, refills it.
Amal enters. He's dressed to ape Jerry, but with a
linen jacket. A lot richer than last seen. From haircut
to shoes there has been a transformation. He is lightly
nervous but breezy with it.

Amal Jerry. Beautiful apartment!

Jerry Shut the fuck up, and where do you get off calling
me by my first name, *you miserable piece of shit*?

Amal faints, crashing over the furniture.

Christ.

(*Shouts.*) Alphonse!

No one comes. Jerry lifts Amal up onto a chair. Amal
is already coming round.

All right.
You need to put your head between your knees.

Amal obeys. Jerry strides back and forth, waiting. He
gestures to, presumably, Alphonse off-stage ('It's
okay'), and continues pacing till Amal sits up, and
makes to stand up.

Sit down. Want to ask you something. What did you pay
for that watch?

Amal Seven grand, sir.

Jerry *Exactly* how much?

Amal Seven thousand, one hundred and forty pounds.

Jerry What do you pay for a haircut?

Amal Eighty including a tip.

Jerry And this is – what? – five years since you came in
with your arse falling out of your trousers, and found

money pouring through the door. Do you know what brings that money through the door?

Amal makes a helpless gesture.

Confidence. Belief.

Amal Can I say something, please?

Jerry No, you can't. You're not here to say anything. (*Taking a folded letter from his pocket.*) You're here to read this and sign it. It says you agree not to look for or accept a job outside the firm for two years, with no salary increase, no bonus, and meanwhile you sit in your corner and share your limp-dick, short-the-market wisdom with nobody except your supervisor – with a sign round your neck saying 'Arsehole', but that's not in the letter. Then maybe you'll think twice before dumping your unbelief with our name on it on a scumbag analyst selling his dope to high-rollers like for example our clients for whom pessimism is the bubonic plague, you brain-dead *quant*. What in fuck's name did you think you were doing?

Amal Getting your attention.

Jerry Well, you got it. Can you stand up?

Amal Yes, sir.

Jerry Then, sign and walk.

Amal takes a fountain pen from his pocket. He talks while he gets the pen ready and signs and folds the letter and gives it back.

Amal Two years? The arsehole sign will be around a lot of people's necks before two years. The market is acting stupid, and the models are out of whack because we don't know how to build a stupid computer. The market is a belief system with a short memory, and it's leveraged on highly correlated billion-dollar bets – and trillions on side-bets – which are going to go wrong together. I mean to *zero*. You pay me for my research.

He gives the folded letter back to Jerry.

Jerry I don't pay you to post it like a fridge magnet on the reception desk.

Amal But I wasn't wrong.

Jerry You were early, which is the same thing.

Amal (*beat*) You're going short the market?

Jerry Use the service stairs.

Amal leaves.

SCENE FIVE

On a screen, Elaine, a young woman, is visibly and audibly reacting to receiving a series of electric shocks. A young Chinese-American woman, Bo, is on hand and speaks to camera.

Bo (*on screen*) How is it, Dr Matthews?

She is talking to Hilary, who is in her small office, watching the screen.
    Hilary is changed: in charge.

Hilary Good.

Cathy walks into the office. Hilary doesn't notice her. Cathy pauses, watching.

Elaine . . . the shocks are coming at regular eight-second intervals, keep an eye on the red light, keep the reactions fairly even, it's your *distress* which increases, not over-dramatic . . .

34

Elaine continues to 'perform'. Hilary notices Cathy,
who is watching the screen. She doesn't know Cathy.

(*Relaxed and friendly.*) Hello.
(*To the screen.*) That's good. Relax.

Hilary turns off the screen.

Who . . . ?

Cathy Is that lady being hurt?

Hilary No. We're playing a trick. It's a . . . kind of game.

Cathy (*puzzled*) Did she know it was a game?

Hilary Yes. She's my friend Elaine. She was pretending.

Cathy Why?

Hilary It's all right. It's what we do here. Sometimes.
We . . . it's difficult to explain.
    My name is Hilary. Hilary Matthews. I don't know
your name.

Cathy It's Cathy.

Pause. Hilary reaches to lift Cathy's 'laminate' on the
cord round her neck, looks at it, lets it fall.
    Leo enters.

Leo Your dad's looking for you.

Cathy runs out.

Hilary Jerry's here . . . ?

Leo He's giving his daughter the tour. She wants all the
animals let out, so he thought he'd better show her we're
nicer to people.

Hilary Oh dear.

Leo (*slightly bitter*) He's come to hand out medals. The
Krohl is going to have the cover of *Nature*, did you know?

35

Hilary (*nods*) It's Ursula's team, working with Stanford – infecting neurons with a photoreceptor. I understood it when she explained it, but not so I could explain it to anybody else. She can get a single brain cell to spike by flashing a blue laser on it.

Leo Mouse brain.

Hilary Yes, a mouse brain.

She detects a put-down in him.

What?

Leo I didn't say anything.

Hilary I won't tell anybody.

Leo I think it's a big step forward in the study of mouse brains.

Hilary (*laughs*) That's mean.

Leo (*shrugs*) They're doing optics with mice and calling it consciousness. A mouse is a bundle of behavioural responses to physical stimuli. Poking it with a stick is the same thing bigger. Light photons hit the retina, smell molecules get the whiskers twitching, and improved technology will show the mechanism all the way to cheese response. It's only amazing, it's not counter-intuitive. But *cognition* – reasoning, imagining, believing . . . that's hard. How does the brain do self-consciousness? – reference? – metaphor? 'I wandered lonely as a cloud.' As a *what*? 'Thy two breasts are like two young roes that are twins, which feed among the lilies.' Like two what which what? That's *hard*. Where is it happening? How? If you had a choice, would you choose a mouse? Would you choose optics? Would you spend your time looking at a brain while you poke it with a laser?

Hilary Not me, boss. It's a no-brainer. The psyche in psychology is Greek for soul.

Leo lets that go by.

Leo You need something with a mind which can talk you through.

He sighs.

Still, the cover of *Nature* is pretty sexy. Do you have anything that sexy? It would do wonders for the department's fitness in the struggle for survival at the Krohl.

Hilary Seriously?

Leo Seriously. The ground is moving under us.

Hilary What would be that sexy?

Leo A predictive theory of human behaviour, for instance. If there were a Nobel Prize for psychology, that would do it. Why are predictions wrong half the time?

Hilary (*roused*) Being wrong about human behaviour half the time is our guiding star, Leo! It's what's telling us the study of the mind is not a science. We're dealing in mind stuff that doesn't show up in a scan – accountability, duty, freewill, *language*, all the stuff that makes behaviour unpredictable.

Leo You're not listening. It's the Jerry Institute for Brain Science, and I'd like to have something that gets his attention before there's a genetic algorithm that will do our job in a computer.

Hilary It won't.

Leo They're working on it.

Hilary It won't compute. At Loughborough we used to do a child custody test. You describe two parents. Parent A is across-the-board average – health, wealth, social life, everything. Parent B is positives and negatives – richer, but travels a lot, great rapport but minor health problems, etcetera. When you ask which parent should be *awarded* custody, you get a fat majority for Parent B. When you ask which parent should be *denied* custody, you get a fat majority for Parent B. It doesn't compute. We did it over and over, and it didn't compute.

Leo You never brought that up at your interview.

Hilary (*laughs*) Leo, do you *remember* my interview?

Leo What do you think of Bo?

Hilary Who? Oh, Bo. I haven't had time to . . .

Leo She's unqualified in psychology, and over-qualified in maths but I've a good feeling about her.

Bo enters, carrying a paper cup of coffee and a sheaf of paper, thirty hand-filled questionnaires.

(*To Bo.*) And here you are.
(*To Hilary.*) Come by later . . . something you might like.

Hilary Oh, yes? What?

Leo (*to Bo*) I'll see you later, too, Bo.

He leaves.

Bo I've got the questionnaires, Dr Matthews.

Hilary Hilary is fine. All done?

Bo Yes. The guinea pigs are doing coffee break.

Hilary (*correcting*) Test subjects. The guinea pigs get lettuce.

Bo Sorry. I brought you one.

She puts the cup down.

Is Elaine a research assistant?

38

Hilary No. That would work if we used real electricity. She's an actor. We're doing a variation of a well-known experiment. The test subjects don't know they're the subject of the experiment. They think Elaine is. I'll fill you in as we go. How did you get on with Leo?

Bo Dr Reinhart? He seemed very nice. I really enjoyed the interview.

Hilary Well, so you know what this day is about.

Bo Well . . . to see if I'm smart, I guess . . .

Hilary No, that's a given. It's to see if you'll be happy here. For you to see, for us to see. We're a small department. Brain science gets most of the building, most of the money, and any glory that's going. Neurobiology, it's king, queen, ugly sisters and golden coach. We don't do brains, we do minds. Three rooms, two teams, one frock and a pumpkin, that's psychology at the Krohl. (*Taking the questionnaires.*) Thank you.

  Hilary dumps the questionnaires into a bin.

Bo Oh . . . !

Hilary We don't look at them. The questionnaires have to be convincing but they're a charade for the benefit of the test subjects. We divide the subjects into two groups randomly. We tell group one they scored high for empathy, we tell group two they scored low for empathy. So, when we get to the experiment we can allow for suggestibility.

Bo One at a time?

Hilary (*nods*) One on one. But we're not testing for empathy.

Bo What, then?

Hilary Motivation. Egoist motives and altruistic motives. Selfish and unselfish. There's a commonsense view that

39

we're selfish by nature, and unselfish when we override our nature, basically by culture. What do you think?

Bo I think it's good to be good, I don't see that it matters what makes you good.

Hilary It might matter if people who are out for themselves think they're justified by biology.

Pause. Hilary sips her coffee.

Bo Yes.

Hilary We're trying to understand other minds, and we don't really understand our own. Why did you bring me this coffee? Perhaps you thought I looked as if I needed some coffee; so that would be an *altruistic* motive. Or perhaps your ultimate motivation was that you wanted to make some sort of good impression; which would be an *egoistic* motive for bringing me a cup of coffee. I could ask you. I could ask a subject who opts to withdraw, 'Is it Elaine's distress or your distress that motivated you?' But how do I know the answer is honest? And if it's honest, how do I know it's reliable? So you don't ask that. You ask something else, to get the answer to the question you didn't ask. You twiddle the knobs on the experiment, like tuning out the static and feedback on an old radio.

Bo has been discomfited. She takes one of the questionnaires from the bin and glances at it.

Bo What do you do with these?

Hilary Shred them . . . confidentiality issues. The data we collect from an experiment is kept anonymous.

Bo . . . A lot of detail here . . . personal detail . . . not to be using it . . .

Hilary The reason we don't look at the questionnaires is, once you look you find the special cases who will skew your precious results. Outliers. But the point is the subjects are a random sample. If you're tempted to weed out the outliers, you're rigging the experiment, and that's a sin. If there's a hidden bias in the design of the experiment the results are not information, they're misinformation, and understanding the human mind is difficult without that, it's like trying to catch a sunbeam in your cupped hands.

Bo You're testing for motivation, one-on-one with Elaine, and you're – what? – adjusting for empathy?

Hilary Yes.

Bo But they don't really feel empathy with *Elaine* –

Hilary They don't know Elaine.

Bo – they're just *told* they scored high or low. On what? Having an empathy-type nature?

Hilary finds herself on the back foot. Her empathy with Bo is cooling rapidly.

Hilary Disposition, yes. What?

Bo It just seems kind of approximate.

Hilary Really?

Bo Empathy-wise, you've made two groups of clones.

Hilary Well . . . how else . . . ?

Bo You can match every subject with their own Elaines, with very high or medium high empathy, or low, whatever.

Hilary (*exasperated*) We haven't got a lot of Elaines . . .!

Bo No, you *describe* Elaine each time different, to fit their questionnaire. There's this one here who's a middle child, so Elaine can be a middle child . . .

Hilary thinks about this. She takes all the questionnaires out of the bin, takes the questionnaire from Bo, and puts them into an empty box-file, which she adds to a row of box-files.

Out of nowhere, Bo bursts into angry tears.

I wasn't doing egoist or altruist anything! The man said to bring you this cup of coffee so I brought you the fucking coffee!

Hilary stays quiet while Bo recovers.

I'm sorry. I don't swear a lot.

Hilary Do you swear in Chinese?

Bo No, never. My grandmother would have killed me.

Hilary Where did you graduate, Bo?

Bo Shanghai and Caltech.

Hilary Shanghai and Caltech.

Bo Then my Master's at Cambridge.

Hilary You . . . ? Really.

Bo Then I got a job offer from Krohl Capital Management . . . I was a quant for a year at Krohl, but . . . well, the money was good, I'll say that, but it wasn't good money, you know?

Hilary *Good* money?

Bo Gaming the market to make more money for people with money.

Hilary Jerry's money was seed money for the Institute, half a billion and counting, so that's good money, isn't it?

Bo He did something good with it. But I'd like to do something good with math without turning math into money first. A friend at KCM said I should try for a psychology doctorate here – a quant, Amal. He knows you.

Hilary Who? Oh. Yes. Amal. Yes, he would do that. Do you see Amal?

Bo Yes. He's . . . who I'm seeing.

Hilary Coincidence.
Did he tell you about us?

Bo Really?

Hilary No – we were both up for this slot.

Bo Oh. And . . . you got it.

Hilary Yes. It was a miracle.

SCENE SIX

In an empty space, Julia is doing a one-on-one pilates session with Hilary. Hilary's mind is not on it.

Julia You're not right.

Hilary Sorry.

Julia Leave your work in the office.

Hilary Yes.
We've got this test going . . . escape options from testing for pain thresholds on a volunteer, that's the story, using electric shocks . . . and Jerry Krohl's daughter walked in on . . .

Julia I didn't know he had a daughter.

Hilary Nor did I, but he does. School-age like Catherine. Her name's Catherine. She saw, she was upset seeing . . . She thought the girl was being tortured. You should have seen her face.

Julia But you explained, didn't you?

43

Hilary Of course. I think so. Yes.

Julia Then why are you holding on to it?

Pause.

It must have happened often enough, girls with the same name.

Hilary You don't get used to it.

Julia I suppose you don't.

Hilary interrupts the exercise and sits up to address Julia directly.

Hilary Julia, can you *remember*?

Julia What?

Hilary The Purple Gang.

Julia Yes.

Hilary We were bullies. Weren't we?

Julia No!
No more than we were bullied!

Hilary We used to gang up on the ones who were . . . you know . . .

Julia Gimpy.

Hilary Gimpy. Peggy Potter was gimpy because her mother knitted her school jumpers. I used to make Gillian Meadows cry because the gang said I had a crush on her, which I did.

Julia Stop it. (*Upset.*) Schoolgirls!

Hilary But who can I trust her with? Who can I trust not to make her cry, flicking her behind the knees with a wet towel like we used to, rampaging through the changing rooms after games?

Julia Buck up, Hilly. If that's Catherine's only problem.

Hilary I missed her like half of me from the first day, and the worst thing was, there was literally nothing I could give her, do for her, she'd just *gone*, and then I thought up something I could do, just to, just to be *good*, so that in return someone, God, I suppose, would look after her.

Julia (*pause*) Do you believe in God?

Hilary I have to.
But I'll tell you what, though. Everyone should say a prayer every day, anyway, for who you love, just because it puts them in your diary. For ages now, I've gone for weeks without thinking of Catherine. Months. I've been letting her go, as though I'd swapped her for a doctorate. Oh, Julia . . .

> *She hugs and holds Julia.*
> *Ursula enters, unfussed, good-humoured.*

Ursula Git yer haynds off mah woman.

Hilary (*disengaging*) Ursula, I need to ask you something. Could the cosmos be teleological?

Ursula Oh, fuck a duck.
No. Why?
(*To Julia.*) Teleological, sweet pea, having a purpose, nothing to do with the telly.

Julia Don't patronise *me*, you dyke, you're on my patch.

Hilary How about panpsychism?

Ursula No. Nature isn't conscious. Trees are not conscious.

Hilary Functionalism?

Ursula No. A thermostat is not even a tiny bit conscious. Have you been reading after lights out?

Hilary What about quantum-level brain processes to explain consciousness?

Ursula She has!

Hilary Will you show me how Gödel's Proof means a brain can't be modelled on a computer?

Ursula You wouldn't know Gödel's Proof if it had suspenders in Selfridge's window.

Hilary Ursula, I need you to show me!

Ursula *Now?*

Hilary No, not *now*. Sundays and evenings, tutorials.

Julia Oh, thanks.

Ursula Why?

Hilary (*excited*) For a conference paper – sort of – with a summer vac stitched on, is what I'm thinking.

Julia Lovely. Where?

Hilary Venice! Leo's giving the status paper for the Krohl, big psycho conference in June, and he blagged them into giving me a place on a round-table on consciousness.

Ursula and Julia catch each other's eye, and stare deadpan at Hilary: 'Wake up! – He wants to bed you.'

What?

She catches on, rolls her eyes.

No way! No way!

SCENE SEVEN

*Venice. Hotel room: a good hotel; a floor-level minibar/
fridge with an interior light.*

*Hilary, wearing a hotel bathrobe, her hair wet from
the shower, is kneeling by the bed, saying her prayers.*

*Sound and spilled light indicate an active shower,
which is soon turned off.*

*Spike enters, wearing an identical bathrobe, wet from
the shower. He is only slightly wrong-footed by seeing
Hilary at her prayers. He begins putting on his pants and
socks. During the scene he puts on the clothes he had
taken off.*

*Hilary stands up. She watches Spike putting on his
shirt.*

Spike So . . . how've you been?

Hilary Have you got a date?

Spike I did have . . . drinks party for UCL's new Nobel,
but it's in the hotel . . . I'll catch what's left of it. I can
come back if you like.

Hilary I'll be asleep. In case I don't see you, good luck
with the physiology of – what? I can't be there. I'll be at
Leo Reinhart's session.

Spike 'The Physiology of High Stakes'. We took saliva
samples at the world poker championship. The cortisol
levels went crazy.

Hilary Is that good? I don't mean *good*.

Spike laughs. A beat.

Spike I haven't heard from you for years.

Hilary I haven't heard from you *at all*.

Spike Really? That's bad.

Hilary (*laughs*) Is the sex better at UCL or Loughborough?

Spike UCL. Or it's to do with being a prof. Won't I see you on the boat?

Hilary Boat?

Spike The Krohl party, it's on Jerry Krohl's boat – an eyesore, frankly, but I had an invitation under my door.

Hilary No, I'm taking off after my round table – Florence, Pisa, Siena . . . on the cheap. Do you want to come?

Spike Don't you have anyone to go with?

Hilary You're anyone.

Spike Hilly.

Hilary Did you read my . . .

Spike Yeah . . . Let me make three points about your pre-print.

> *The pre-print is twenty pages, self-published. Spike takes it out of his jacket, and enumerates his points with his spare fingers.*

Don't circulate it.
    If you circulate it, don't put your name on it.
    If you put your name on it, don't put the Krohl's name on it.

> *An afterthought.*

Four points. If you circulate it with your name and the Krohl's name on it, don't call it 'Is God the Last Man Standing?'

Hilary Why?

Spike Because it will make you unemployable. You'd have to do philosophy.

Hilary I haven't written anything which isn't in plain sight. Materialism is in trouble, and we're all materialists now. Everything is matter. There is no science that says beauty is truth or truth beauty, but the gondolas are heaving with name-tagged materialists having their minds blown by Venice. What is to be done with the sublime if you're proud to be a materialist? To save the appearance of value, no theory is too unlikely, no idea too far-out to float so long as it sounds like science – elementary particles with teeny-weeny consciousness; or a cosmos with attitude; or the life of the mind as the software of a biological computer. These are desperate measures, Spike! What does materialism remind you of? It's a faith.

Spike But it's pathetic to rely on a supreme being to underwrite what you call your values. Why are you afraid of making your own?

Hilary You don't claim to make your own. What's the difference between a supreme being and being programmed by your biology?

Spike Freedom. I can override the programming.

Hilary Who can? Who's the 'you' outside your brain? *Where?*

Spike I wish I'd pulled that primatologist with the thigh boots who was hitting on me at registration. Why don't you leave me alone?
  At least change the title, will you?

Hilary All right.

Spike At least. But you didn't write these equations, I know that much.

Hilary I might have done.

Spike No, not these. You shagged a mathematician.

Hilary No, I didn't. But there's a Chinese girl in the department who's phenomenal. She was a quant at KCM before.

Spike Krohl's hedge-fund? That's a comedown.

Hilary She doesn't think so. I'm mad about her, actually. She's designed an experiment like nothing in the literature – ninety-six kids in four age groups –

Spike (*quite impressed*) Ninety-six?

Hilary Close to, probably. We've got pretty much an entire school participating, thanks to Jerry.
   So you liked her equations?

Spike I liked them, but they're not tied into hard data.

Hilary They show there isn't enough geological time for the living world to have been selected-out by chance mutations.

Spike Really? Look around. You're just hung up on your personal incredulity.

Hilary (*roused*) Well, where's yours? Someone tells you you can run the film backward billions of years to an enormous bang and nothing but particles joining up into big clumps like this one, except not like this one – because on this one the chemistry came alive and kicked into an algorithm that kept unspooling till there was you collecting spit from a poker game, and you don't bat an eyelid.

Spike Yup. Love it. Now do God, and see which one of us looks credulous.
   I went to Pisa once, a conference, by EasyJet. The control tower was a disappointment; a missed branding opportunity, one felt.
   You wouldn't want someone hanging on to your skirts who thinks when you've seen one town in Tuscany you've seen them all.

I wouldn't know what to do with myself if there's no conference. I get antsy if there isn't a new journal to look at every day.

Hilary I thought you were going to the party.

Spike Do you mind if I change my mind?

Hilary Why? You're not going to spoil everything by worrying about me, are you? Anyway, don't you want to meet the Nobel Laureate?

Spike I met him, he's a force-of-nature type who's realised he can act modest now: it's quite irritating.

Hilary All right, but I'm going to sleep.

Spike, dressed now, starts getting undressed. Hilary takes off her robe and puts on a T-shirt nightgown.

Spike Still saying our prayers, are we? Still God, is it?

Hilary Whoever's up for it. I wish you'd stop saying 'God' like that, as if I'm talking about someone who created the world in six days and then had a rest. He'd think I was a complete idiot. But there are things we believe are right or wrong like, say, torturing someone with electric shocks, and if this belief is also a brain-state, that's fine by me, but our brain-state is *about* something, it's about torture, which is right or wrong whether we're thinking about it or not.

Spike You don't need God for that.

Hilary (*forcefully*) But you need *something* for it to be true, some kind of overall moral intelligence, otherwise we're just marking our own homework. That's what I pray to for Catherine, because somewhere between ape-men and the beginning of religion, we became aware of an enormous fact we didn't understand.

Spike We did. Its name was death. Who's Catherine?

Hilary Oh, sorry. I thought I told you. She's my daughter.

Spike You haven't got a daughter. Have you?

Hilary Yes. She'll be thirteen in November.

Spike *Thirteen?* So . . .

Hilary Fifteen.

Spike What?

Hilary I was fifteen.

Spike God, Hil. Where is she?

Hilary (*shrugs*) Catherine was possibly the last 'shame' baby. Nowadays the babies are mostly taken away from mothers who neglect them or can't cope, but shame is pretty much extinct. When she's eighteen she can ask to see her birth certificate. If she wants to. If she knows she's adopted.

Spike Oh, Hil. I'm sorry.

Hilary Thanks.

She gets into bed and turns off her bedside light, leaving the room dimly lit. Pause.

Would you do something for me, Spike?

Spike Anything.

Hilary Promise?

Spike Should I get dressed or undressed?

Hilary Will you, though?

Spike Yes. Okay. Sure. What?

Hilary Will you say a prayer?

Spike (*pause*) What?

Hilary Pray for her. Just for a moment.

Spike No. You mean like pray-to-God pray?
  No. Why?

Hilary Just because. If you, of all people, if *even you* . . .

Spike No. I mean . . . Hilly . . . it would be meaningless, wouldn't it?

Hilary I don't know. That would be up to you.

Spike It wouldn't be up to me. It just *is* meaningless.

Hilary If it's meaningless, what's your problem?

Spike I'd be betraying everything I believe in.

Hilary And that's a problem, is it?

  Pause.

Spike Is that why you pray for forgiveness?

Hilary Did I tell you that? I just want to be allowed to *know*, to stop imagining, and I pray for her . . . 'Please God let Catherine be all right. Please God let her parents be kind to her . . .'

Spike Oh. So what happened to 'Please Overall Moral Intelligence'? Aren't you embarrassed?

Hilary Yes.

  She gets out of bed and goes into the bathroom.

(*Leaving.*) Do you want something from the minibar?

Spike (*to himself*) The *minibar?*

  He hears the shower turning full on.

(*Calls.*) You already had . . . Are you having a shower?

  She closes the bathroom door. Spike goes to the minibar and crouches to look at the miniatures in the

53

*door, then moves the larger bottles around, kneeling to
look at the bottles in the back. He finds a bottle of
beer, examines the label. He listens to the noise of the
water.*

(*Calls.*) You're crying in the shower. Aren't you? I know
you are.

*He pauses to listen, kneeling in the light from the
minibar.*

SCENE EIGHT

Hilary's office.
    *Bo stands by (sits) while Hilary reads what she scrolls
up on her desk computer.*
    *Hilary is impressed, excited, astonished, and half
disbelieving.*
    *Bo has just received a holiday gift, a necklace, and is
in the act of unwrapping the box.*

Bo It's lovely. Thank you!

*She puts the necklace on. Hilary ignores her, her
attention captured by the scrolling screen. After a few
more moments, she sits back. Pause. Bo watches her
expectantly, shyly.*

Hilary Has Leo seen this?

Bo I wanted you to see it first.

Hilary Quite right. I'll want to go through the raw data,
all of it, and to be taken through the maths.

Bo It checks out. The mathematics is basic.

Hilary This is bloody sensational. But I wish you'd
waited for me, Bo. No offence, but we're going to have to
be bulletproof, immaculate.

Bo I was ready. The kids were ready.

Hilary Well, it's great. Eighty-eight kids is damned good.

Bo And I wanted it for you when you came back.

Hilary You . . . ?

Leo enters, holding pages of email.

Leo. Beautiful day.

Leo (*cold*) Fuck the beautiful day. What do you call this, and why has it got our name on it?

An awkward pause. Bo leaves.

Hilary You mean my Venice discussion paper?

Leo Yes, I mean your Venice discussion paper, which is the subject of several emails from the comedians among my friends and colleagues. We do science here, Hilary!

Hilary This is about science, the psychology of the scientific mind-set.

Leo Psychology of bullshit. It's about God.

Hilary It's about the Hard Problem. It says every theory proposed for the problem of consciousness has the same degree of demonstrability as divine intervention. So psychologically – they're equivalent.

Leo What it says is that if you're an atheist, you're in denial.

Hilary (*patiently*) No, it says we may be in denial about mind–body dualism.

Leo Oh, well, that takes care of the Hard Problem! The reason it's *hard*, you pig's arse, is that mind–body is the problem!

His emotion spent, he sits down heavily.

I could have done without this at the minute. Welcome back, I think. Sorry about my language.

Pause.

Also me in Venice. I apologise.

Hilary I took it as a compliment, Leo.
    Has something happened?

Leo I think so. The Krohl is taking on another behavioural psychologist, starting September.

Hilary Well . . . that's good, isn't it?

Leo He's not coming to my department. He'll have an office in Biochem.

Hilary Who's paying for him? Is he on our budget?

Leo No.

Hilary That's . . . not so good.

Leo I'm impressed you understand. If you hadn't outed yourself as a Cartesian dualist you could have ended up as a head of department. But you get the message. Psychology as an enterprise is on its way out, is what they're telling us. We're on a countdown to the embedded brain answering all the questions about the disembodied mind.

Hilary What's his angle, this . . . ?

Leo Hormone-related performance in human subjects.

Hilary Hormone-related performance? Like what?

Leo Like working on the trading desk at KCM. Am I going too fast for you?

Hilary (*after a beat*) No.

Leo Jerry is smitten.

Hilary I can see. Where did all this . . .?

Leo On his boat.

Hilary His *boat*?

Leo Jerry read this man's paper in Venice. The paper was nothing to do with the financial market, it was poker players –

Hilary takes this in without a flicker.

– but Jerry got it in one: it was about risk-taking and risk-aversion. So he invited Spencer to the Krohl party.

Hilary Spencer?

Leo His name is Spencer something.

A reflexive laugh from Hilary.

It was a love match, Jerry in a yachting cap, and Spencer. A trading desk is next up.

Hilary I'm trying to follow the money. Where's the money?

Leo The financial models assume a trader's appetite for risk is a stable trait, like the colour of his eyes but, according to Spencer, not so. It's not intellectual, it's the body, the current state of his body. Stress releases a cocktail of hormones. By getting your traders to spit into a paper cup, you can predict who'll get risk-happy in a market he thinks he understands, and lose his gains; or, contrariwise, predict who will be paralysed by risk-aversion in a roller-coaster market where there's money to be made. Do we like this? We adore it. It monetises the hormonal state of your trading desk!

Hilary Gosh.

Leo So it's behavioural but I'll be damned if it's psychology. There are people here who wonder why we're in the building. Jerry isn't one of them, so far, but it's a long time since the department published anything that went viral. For Jerry that's like trading at a loss.

Hilary returns to her computer.

Hilary Do you want to see something sexy?

SCENE NINE

Hilary's flat.
A dinner party is well under way, though there is no dinner as yet, and no dinner table as such, only a finger-food first course on a coffee table, around which, more or less at floor level, sit Ursula, Julia, Spike and Amal, who is opening a bottle of champagne.
Bo has gone 'outside' to a notional balcony or patio, to smoke a cigarette, and is visible, withdrawn into herself.
It is not a successful dinner party. The hostess – Hilary, temporarily out of sight in the kitchen – is trying too hard, and has no talent for cooking. Amal has not met Spike, Ursula or Julia before; Amal and Spike have not met each other, and their better sides are unknown to each other. They have not taken to each other, and Spike is getting drunk, which increases his fluency but doesn't improve his charity. Ursula is not trying hard to help things along. Julia is doing her good-natured best. As a couple, Amal and Bo are at odds with each other.
The four already have glasses for the wine they are drinking, the bottle in evidence.

Amal That's a very good question.

He pops the cork. Glasses are emptied down throats to receive the champagne. Amal empties his almost full glass carelessly into a potted flower which still has its gift-wrapping around it.

I don't think I've ever been asked this question before. In fact, you may be the first person who's ever asked it. Congratulations, Julia! So, yes indeed, what exactly *is* a hedge fund?

Julia Sorr-ee!

Ursula Well, I don't know what a hedge-fund does. Do you, Spike?

Spike Yes.

Ursula Go on, then.

Spike No. I want to see if Amal knows.

Amal What? But I work in a hedge-fund!

Spike I prefer to be the judge of that.

Julia But I really want to know.

Spike Well, let's say you have ten million pounds which you'd like to put to work. You decide to invest it in Krohl Capital Management. First, Jerry Krohl takes two per cent per year, £200,000, as his fee for taking your money to gamble with. Then he gambles with it, and he keeps twenty per cent of the winnings. If he loses, the losses are all yours.

Amal (*mock-impressed*) Do you work in a hedge-fund?

Bo wanders in and sits herself where she has left her glass of cola.

Ursula But why would anyone . . . Could you explain what you actually spend your day doing?

Amal Do I have to? I don't ask you about pilates. No offence.

Ursula None taken.

Julia It's me who does pilates. You can ask me.

59

Amal With pilates, it's very difficult to think of anything to ask.

Julia (*humbly*) I suppose so.

Ursula (*to Bo*) Dump him.

Bo has noticed the spillage of wine over the flowering plant.

Bo What have you done to my flower? Honestly.

Bo separates the plant from its paper, screws up the paper and chucks it at Amal.

Spike He spends his day staring at – how many computer screens is it, Amal?

Amal Call it seven.

Spike Seven. That would be stocks, bonds, commodities, currencies, pornography, Sky Sports and emails.

Julia It doesn't explain why anyone would give him their money.

Spike Amal?

Amal Because Krohl Capital Management averaged sixteen per cent per annum return on capital. Averaged. After expenses.
(*To Julia.*) That's a lot.

Julia (*snaps*) Yes, I do know that.

Bo The ultimate motivation is that banking regulations don't apply to hedge-funds. In fact, getting round the rules is the reason for hedge-funds. Like Basel rules for capital reserves.

Amal I could explain that, but I decline. First it's Basel rules, and before you know where you are, it's arbitrage, leverage, securitisation . . . I refuse.

Bo Amal doesn't mean to be rude.

Ursula Something's burning.

Bo He's embarrassed.

Hilary enters with food and plates, etc. Bo jumps up to help her. Space is made on the table. And so on.

Hilary Sorry it's a bit overdone. Everyone help yourself. Give me a glass, someone . . . Oh, who brought that beautiful flower? . . . Bo, thank you! And champagne . . .

Spike commandeers the bottle, examining the label.

Spike What does this cost, Amal?

Amal That is so crass. A hundred quid.

Hilary Pay attention a minute. This evening is for Bo . . . and –

She waves the journal triumphantly.

– *The Journal of Cognitive Studies*! To Bo's first publication! Has everyone got a glass?

Bo (*to Hilary, shyly*) Thank you.
Mine is not the only name on this paper.

Hilary Only the first.

Bo You all understand, there would be no paper without Hilary.

Hilary Not true. This is Bo's paper, it's her experiment, and it's going to cause a stir.

Ursula (*with the journal*) It doesn't look good if the authors are getting out from under. Let me. The toast is ' "Ultimate Goods". B. Sheng-Tsu and H.J. Matthews'.

General toasting.

Hilary Done. Eat.

Dinner proceeds tentatively. Spike doesn't eat.

Spike Did Leo Reinhart ask to see the raw data?

Hilary Do you really think he wouldn't? He called it a beautiful experiment.

Spike A work of art.

Hilary (*mildly*) Oh, shut up, Spencer.

Julia What sort of stir will it cause, Hilly?

Hilary The sort where an experiment comes up with the wrong answer for a lot of people.

Spike Especially when it's the wrong answer to its own question.

Hilary Spike is the sceptic at the feast, but Bo and I don't care. I'm sorry about the feast, though. Don't eat it. I'm so sorry, Bo.

Julia It's really tasty.

Bo I don't mind.

Ursula Interesting. Was the recipe in *Cognitive Studies*?

Amal There's a certain sort of absent-mindedness about it, you mean?

Hilary Oh, bugger it!

She leaps into action, snatching everyone's plate away, against half-hearted protests.

Cheese! Cheese and biscuits, coffee and I've baked a cake!

Bo I'll help you. Don't worry about it.

In a couple of beats, Hilary and Bo have left with the debris.
Spike has made no attempt to eat, but has helped himself to the champagne.

Ursula looks at the journal.

Ursula 'Ultimate Goods' . . . Hilary makes altruism sound as if it has something to do with morality.

Spike She was always like that.

Julia Doesn't it mean being good?

Ursula No.

Julia Well, it's probably because she *is* good.

Ursula How do you work that out?

Julia I didn't work it out.

Ursula Well, shut up, then.

Julia is hurt.

Oh, dear.

She hugs Julia, who resists.

Amal (*to Julia*) Altruism just means increasing someone else's fitness at the expense of your own.

Spike Now you're making it sound as if it's got something to do with pilates.

Julia (*bursts out*) And you shut up, too!

Spike So sorry.
(*To Ursula.*) Tell her about vampire bats.

Ursula I'll tell you the miracle of the brain worm, that'll cheer you up. There's a parasite that lives inside a cow. The eggs come out with the cowpat. Problem: how does the parasite get back inside the cow to complete its life cycle? First, the eggs get eaten by a snail, and develop inside the snail before being ejected in a mucus; which is eaten by ants. About fifty of the tiny creatures are now inside an ant. They bore a hole in the stomach wall, and one of the fifty works its way up into the brain of the ant. This is the brain worm. It changes the behaviour of the ant, causing the ant to obsessively climb up to the tip of a blade of grass over and over again, thus increasing the ant's chances of being eaten by a cow. But the brain worm's life is over. Now, that's what I call altruism.

Julia Well, I don't! It's horrible.

Hilary and Bo return with cheese, biscuits, etc. which they set down.

Hilary Stilton!

Julia Ugh! – No thanks!

Hilary What are we talking about?

Spike About you, of course.
(*To Ursula.*) Did you read it? It's a corker. Eighty-eight kids in a sort of creative writing class with alternate-choice modules scored for egoist/altruist values . . . which shows, or is supposed to show, or could be said to show when held up to a strong light, that six-year-olds are nicer than eight-year-olds, who are nicer than ten-year-olds, who are nicer than twelve-year-olds.

Hilary It does show that.

Spike Which, our authors conclude, points to a strong indication that we start off nice and learn to be nasty, instead of the received wisdom that we start off nasty and learn to be nice. *Ergo*, good, or ultimate niceness, has its root in nature. Or rather human nature. Or rather human nature from when it separated from animal nature, which is actually a problem for people like me who can't see the join. Does H. J. Matthews think it happened in earthquake, wind and fire?

Hilary (*coldly*) Feel free, Spike.

Spike And, by the way Fig. 3, showing an orderly transition from niceness to nastiness, gives off, if you don't mind me saying so, a distinct whiff of week-old fish.

Bo (*shocked*) Excuse me?

Hilary (*grim*) I'm going to get the coffee. Don't imagine for a moment you're staying the night.

Hilary goes back to the kitchen.

Spike I didn't like the sound of that.
(*To Bo.*) I suppose a fuck is out of –

Amal (*objecting*) Hey!

Ursula I don't think you should drink any more.

Spike Sorry, have I given offence? Last thing on my mind. Sorry.
(*To Bo.*) Terribly sorry.
(*To Julia.*) I don't suppose . . . No.

Julia I think you should eat something.

Spike Is that your best offer?

He finds something funny. He starts laughing to himself. He can't stop laughing, until Ursula walks across to him and punches him in the face, knocking him over. Ursula goes back to her seat.

Amal (*to Bo*) To be fair to Spike, I actually understood your paper, the way he explained it. I'm going to read it again. I never got to the end.

Bo gives him a stare.

Bo I'm going to have a cigarette.

She goes 'outside'.

Ursula (*to Amal*) Nice one.

Spike suddenly sits up, glazed.

Spike I think my cortisol count has gone through the roof.

Hilary enters with a coffee tray.

Ah! Coffee! Can I help?

Hilary No.

Amal (*to Hilary*) I've been trying to imagine everyone I work with as eight-year-olds.

Hilary Really? Why?

Amal Trying to imagine them as nice little boys and girls. The thing about the market is, it consists entirely of transactions between egoists. An altruistic trader, salesman, broker, customer . . . I mean, forget black swans, we're talking African polar bears.

Hilary So?

Amal I can't imagine them sharing their toffees with each other.

Spike I did. Opal Fruits . . . Opal Fruits are the Ultimate Goods of confectionery.

He is ignored.

Hilary Where's Bo?

Julia Went outside for a smoke.

Hilary She doesn't have to do that.

Outside, where Bo is smoking, there is the distant noise and illumination of modest fireworks.

Spike Julia is the Opal Fruit of pilates.

Hilary (*to Julia*) Could you pour the coffee for me?

Hilary and Julia have a moment of intimacy.

Julia Are you all right, Hilly?

Hilary Yes. Guess what? I burnt her cake, too.

66

Hilary is close to tears. She goes outside. The fireworks continue sporadically, and stop.

You'd never have guessed it's my first dinner party.

Bo looks at her closely.

Bo Are you crying?

Hilary Fireworks make me cry.

Bo It doesn't matter about the dinner.

Bo puts her arm tentatively around Hilary. Hilary allows herself to be comforted for a moment, then disengages.

Is Spike your boyfriend?

Hilary I hope not.

Bo Why is he being like that?

Hilary Because he is like that. We never agree about anything.

Bo You don't seem to care what he said . . . about the paper.

Hilary I don't. He said a lot more before you turned up. I'm used to Spike.

Bo What sort of lot more?

Hilary The same sort. But I went through the data with a toothcomb, and the paper is solid. Don't lose confidence, Bo.

Bo (*bursts out*) I wish it wasn't published! I didn't do it for it to be in some journal where anyone can . . .

Hilary That's silly. Publication is how you get on. Sometimes it gets to be a rough-house, but that's part of the game.

Bo I think I may have done something bad.

Hilary (*pause*) Like what?

Bo There were ninety-six children to start with.

Hilary Well . . . okay. But you went with eighty-eight. Right? Eighty-eight participated.

Bo No, they all did.

Hilary (*pause*) But . . . wait . . . they all ninety-six participated? And – what? – eight kids didn't stay the course, so you crunched the data for the rest – is that right?

Bo No, I did the math across all ninety-six.

Hilary And then what?

Bo Then I eliminated eight kids, and did the math again.

Hilary Then what?

Bo Then I showed you. When you got back from Italy.

Pause.

Hilary How did you choose the ones you eliminated? Was it random?

Pause.

(*Quietly.*) Shit.
    You took out two from each group who were spoiling your result.

Bo They were freak results!

Hilary They were outliers, Bo! That's what random does, that's why experiments tend not to come out with every hair in place!
    How can you be so stupid? Why did you do it?

Bo How can *you*?

68

Belatedly, Hilary catches up.

Hilary Bo . . . ?

Bo I wanted to give you what would please you!

Hilary (*unmoved*) Yes. But ultimately, you wanted what you wanted, Bo.
It's my fault. I missed it.

Bo (*in tears*) I'm sorry . . .

Bo hurries back indoors. Hilary stays outside.
Indoors, the group is focused on Amal. He is flourishing the almost empty champagne bottle, swigging from it.

Amal I'm good. I've been sitting on my hands for a year watching the market bet on water flowing uphill and flying pigs farting Chanel No. 5. I have to hold my mouth straight to stop laughing, because I'm the official arsehole and it's all starting to look good for Amal. I don't trade. I don't pitch. I work on the computer models which are supposed to manage risk. So long as the market is correcting itself, the models look as if they're working. In theory, the market is a stream of rational acts by self-interested people; so risk ought to be computable, and the models can be proved mathematically to crash about once in the lifetime of the universe. But every now and then, the market's behaviour becomes irrational, as though it's gone mad, or fallen in love. It doesn't compute. It's only computers compute.

He drains the bottle.

So I'm thinking about that.

Hilary's office.
Leo comes in, carrying a folder, containing all the raw
data from the experiment. He dumps it on Hilary's desk,
sits down, sighs. Hilary waits.

Leo Did you think of keeping quiet?

Hilary No.

Leo Did she?

Hilary I'm very, very sorry, Leo.

Leo I'm sorry, too. The data sheets for ninety-six test
subjects. It took me a while to work it out. You can't get
there by taking out two from each group. With group
one, the youngest kids, you have to eliminate the three at
the high end for egoism, selfish little bastards. With
group four, the oldest kids, you eliminate the one at the
high end for altruism, annoying little Mother Teresa.
With the two middle groups, you have to eliminate from
both ends and further in, or the curve goes back on itself.

Pause. Hilary waits.

Start with Bo, then. I'll talk her down, she can have some
paid leave, but she's toast.

Hilary I'm the principal investigator.

Leo That's a title, not a fact. Necessarily. You were in
Italy for nearly three weeks.

Hilary What are you talking about? It's my paper.

Leo Bo is first-author.

Hilary And I'm senior author. I'm mentoring her. She's
one year in, and I gave her first author as a gesture

because she works hard, and I like her, I wanted to encourage her – but it's my paper.

Leo It was her show, though, wasn't it?

Hilary No, it's mine. She contributed, she did a decent job caretaking, but it was all ready to go. There isn't a line in the paper which didn't come across my desk. I *wrote the paper*!

Leo So which of you took out eight –

Hilary I did. (*Beat.*) I cleared it. After she . . . What's the difference? What we're discussing here is Bo, and whether you're going to drag down with me a beginner who took a big pay cut to work here, and had nothing in the paper I didn't sign off on. She was milking the family buffalo when she was eight, and she's the best mathematician in the house. Do you want to lose her? She can survive this. If you fire her over a retracted publication, she won't get a job in *China*.

Leo (*pause*) Why? Why are you wasting my time with this fan dance? Are you in love with her?

Beat.

Hilary She's in love with me.

Leo (*taken aback*) Well! Finally, something I understand.

Pause.

All right.

Hilary All right what?

Leo All right.

Hilary Thank you.

Leo She gets a formal warning.

Hilary Thank you.

Leo All right.

Hilary Thank –

Leo Stop saying that. It's you I don't want to lose.

Hilary I'm going back to school.

Leo What does that mean?

Hilary I want to do a degree course. Philosophy.

Leo Don't get ahead of yourself, Hilly. There's some wiggle-room here –

Hilary I'm retracting a paper from a major journal with the Krohl Institute's name on it.

Leo A correction, not a retraction. An addendum, not a correction.

Hilary You're not seeing straight, Leo. I'm packing. Watch your own back is my advice.

Leo (*beat*) Jerry said the paper was wrong.

Hilary He read it?

Leo It pissed him off that his daughter's group scored low on nice, and high on not so nice. He said Cathy was the nicest person in his family.

Hilary You'd think Jerry would approve of a bit of egoism in his genes.

Leo His genes don't come into it – Cathy's adopted.

Hilary (*pause*) Since when?

Leo Since *when*? She's twelve, I think.

Hilary Does she know?

Leo Jerry's wife is Japanese, so – probably.

Hilary Oh.
    Do you know Catherine's birthday?

72

Leo No, why?

He gets up to leave.

I'd like to tell him his daughter was eliminated for being too nice, but with the data sheets being coded, and the questionnaires shredded . . .

Hilary We don't shred them now.

A beat. She stands up.

She's thirteen.

Leo You don't? Why not?

She walks calmly to the box-files.

Hilary In case they're useful. Leave the data sheets . . . I'll cross-reference . . .

Hilary finds the right box.

Leo (*nods*) I'll wait to call Jerry. Listen . . .

Hilary digs into the box-file among several generations of sheaves of filled-in questionnaires.

I'm going to have to write you a formal letter. Transparency. It's a damnable thing, and I'm sorry about it, I can't tell you how sorry.

Hilary continues searching.

Hilary Thank you.

Leo leaves.
Hilary finds the sheaf, and brings it to her desk.
Hilary finds Cathy's questionnaire, and stares at it.
She lays it down.

(*Mutters.*) Thank you.

Hilary's office.
    *Hilary and Jerry. Hilary is looking for things to put
into a cardboard box too capacious for them.*

Jerry (*on his mobile phone*) Billy, I got your pitch, but
with respect, you arseholes, if you haven't got the
liquidity to pay your debts, why would I want to own
your loan book . . . ?

    He ends the call.

Sorry.

Hilary Is something happening?

Jerry Uh-huh. Reality. Reality so far out on the
distribution curve, it wasn't supposed to be possible.
(*Shrugs.*) But that's where Cathy was, too . . . an outlier.
Do you think it's nature or nurture that's responsible for
Cathy?

Hilary You brought her up – is altruistic behaviour a big
thing with you and Mrs Krohl?

Jerry Well, if philanthropy counts for anything . . .

Hilary I'd need to test you for ultimate motivation.

    Jerry concedes that, wryly amused by her.

Jerry On the other hand, you doing your best to bring
Leo's department down around his ears sounds more like
egoism to me.

Hilary It was irrational.

    Jerry's phone burps. He takes the call.

Jerry (*to phone*) *Guten Tag*, Hans . . . stop, talk slower . . .
I'm sorry, that is tough . . . I can't trade it on, Hans,

there's no one taking the other side of the trade ... Yeah, good luck.

He ends the call and takes a new one.

Charlie . . .? (*Pause.*) Eat it, or default – let me know.

He ends the call.

Hilary What *is* happening?

Jerry A fire sale.

Hilary Why?

Jerry Well . . . a lot of people were selling fire insurance on a house that was burning.

Hilary But not you?

Jerry No. I was buying it.
Cathy and I are going to the country. Would you like to come out to the car?

Hilary I don't think so. Thanks. Did I thank you for keeping her name? I meant to, in my letter.

Jerry You did. Mika liked the name. She said to say, you'd be welcome to visit . . .

Hilary That's very kind. Perhaps when I'm back . . .

Jerry From where?

Hilary NYU, I hope.

Jerry You'll be in New York for . . .?

Hilary Three years, anyway. There's someone teaching philosophy there whose ideas are . . . undemonstrable.

Pause.

Jerry Are you sure?

Hilary Yes, I'm sure.

Jerry Thank you.

Philosophy? Well, serves you right.

We didn't make a drama out of adoption and she hasn't made a drama out of it. But if she asks, of course we'll tell her what we know, and then it's up to her.

Hilary Yes, that's best.

Jerry If you change your mind . . .

Hilary I'll try not to.

The very last thing I imagined was that Catherine was a rich kid.

Jerry Well, what would you rather? She's hit an awkward age – I mean, she's normal, don't imagine she's a saint.

Hilary I don't.

Jerry So. Have you got any money?

Hilary How much do you need?

Jerry Ha.

Hilary I'm fine. I am so fine. I've been carrying my own weather all these years. It's like the first day of spring. You know it's a miracle, don't you?

Jerry A miracle? No. A coincidence. I don't believe in miracles. As a matter of fact, I don't believe in coincidence either. You didn't have the information.

Cathy barges in. She is changed. She has breasts, and street-cred clothes, hair and attitude, currently a mutinous show of fatigue – her boredom performance.

Cathy Dad, I am *so bored* waiting . . .

Jerry Perfect. This is Dr Matthews.

Cathy I know. Hi.

Jerry We're going.

Hilary How are you, Cathy?

Cathy I'm good.

Jerry We're gone. Goodbye.

He answers his phone.

Hey, David . . .

Cathy 'Bye.

Hilary Goodbye.

Jerry (*to phone*) Sorry to hear that . . . a one-chance-in-a-million event . . . A *trillion?* Really?

Jerry and Cathy leave. Hilary stays still, happy. Jerry comes back almost immediately with Cathy's security laminate on its cord, with her small photo on it. He gives it to Hilary, and is walking out again without a pause. He is still on the phone.

(*Entering and leaving.*) . . . If your model was telling you the market was going to do this once every four billion years, David, there's probably something wrong with your . . . Yeah . . .

Jerry has gone. Hilary looks at Cathy's photo.
  Hilary becomes active . . . turning out the drawers in her desk, looking for personal possessions to put into the box. When she has put in a few small items – a book, a sweater, Cathy's security pass – she looks around hopelessly and empties the box on to her desk. She puts the sweater over her shoulders, everything else into her shoulder-bag, and leaves.

The End.